Copy   MW01325402

All rights reserved. No part of this publication may be reproduced, distributed, or transmitted in any form or by any means, including photocopying, recording, or other electronic or mechanical methods, without the prior written permission of the publisher, except in the case of brief quotations embodied in critical reviews and certain other noncommercial uses permitted by copyright law. For permission requests, write to the publisher, at the address below.

ISBN: 979-8-9859522-0-9 (Hardback)

Any references to historical events, real people, or real places are used fictitiously. Names, characters, and places are products of the author's imagination.

Front cover image by David Kasneci.
Book design by David Kasneci.

Printed by Palmetto Publishing, Alpha Graphics, Metro Webb, Bind-Rite in the United States of America.

First printing edition 2021.

David Kasneci
243 Broadway #9188 SMB #11120
Newark, NJ 7104.

www.369project.com

DISCLAIMER

THE CONTENT OF THIS BOOK IS FOR INFORMATION AND EDUCATIONAL PURPOSES ONLY. This book may offer health, fitness, or similar information (including, without limitation, information concerning self-realization exercises, sungazing, earthing, and grounding), but such information is intended for educational and informational purposes only. Neither the author nor publisher makes any representations as to the safety of the practices set forth in this book. If you have questions or concerns, please consult a licensed medical professional. The practices discussed in this book should not be taken as medical or health advice.

Project 369 - Manifestation Planner

Before We Begin, Please Answer The Following Question...

Why Did You Get This Planner?

Every day, before filling out the planner, I would like you to read why you got it in the first place. It will ultimately remind you to reaffirm who you are and where you're going when days aren't the way you desire them to be. It is no coincidence that you received this planner. Either someone told you about it, you heard about it, you got it gifted, or you happen to come across it. The Divine bridge of incidents led you to read this page at this very moment. Congratulations. I'll tell you now that creation is finished. You are exactly where you're supposed to be, here and now. Life is unfolding for you to be able to express your highest potential. We need you to express yourself as the individualization of the Universe that you are. Thank yourself for making the decision to include this habit in your daily life. I am proud of you. This is just the beginning of something amazing. Let us now create miracles.

Manifestation Planner

This planner was created for you to align yourself with your desires. Prior to proceeding, it is critical to acknowledge that you will be taken through a deep phase of revaluing and expanding your beliefs. The reason for this is that a change in belief is a change in reality, whether the change is good or bad. As Dr. Joseph Murphy said, "The law of life is the law of belief."

Prior to manifesting anything in your life, you must cultivate te consciousness of being the person that attains it. This means that your belief system must be in alignment with the belief system required for the life you desire. Now, you may say, "How can I believe in something that is not true?" "How can I believe I am the person I want to be if reality tells me otherwise?"

Well, that is the point. You create it all through your beliefs. You must change seeing is believing to believing is seeing, for the evidence you see in your physical reality is but a reflection of the beliefs that manifested it. Once you change your beliefs about your outer world, without needing to see the physical evidence of it, then your world will have no option but to change accordingly.

You're manifesting at all moments of time, and whether you believe it or not, your state of consciousness, or belief system, is continuously projecting your physical reality.

With this new understanding of the nature of reality, you will now be guided to prompts that will revalue and expand your beliefs. If you wish to answer them appropriately, you are required to cultivate a strong desire to be transformed and reborn.

Self-Concept / Higher-Self

Your self-concept consists of how you consciously view yourself based on what you believe to be true. Your self-concept contains the aspects of yourself that you are fully aware of, and doesn't include the unconscious aspects of yourself that are hidden but still expressed. Many times, others will need to reflect the unconscious qualities and aspects of yourself in order for these aspects to be brought to your conscious awareness and cause you to be aware of them in yourself. Such is the origin of the quote: "Everything and everyone is YOU pushed out."

Being aware of your current beliefs is synonymous with being aware of your environment and surroundings. What you currently experience in your world is but a reflection of your beliefs about yourself. What you say "I AM" to is externalized automatically, without effort or will. Your world is nothing more than your conditioned mind objectified.

As we change our beliefs about ourselves, our thoughts and behaviors follow, and our reality conforms. I endeavor to have you develop a belief system in harmony with your vision.

On the next page, we will ask you questions that will cause you to identify the qualities, behaviors, and feelings associated with your higher self. You will be required to visualize this person and explain it in the following box. Imagine what qualities you would have, how you would feel, and how you would habitually behave. Commit to being this version of yourself every day, and aim to visualize, feel, and express this person daily. Don't wait for "the time to be right," for the only time that exists is now.

Self-Concept / Higher-Self

Ways to Change Your Life

- Wake up at the same time everyday
- Go to sleep at the same time everyday
- Meditate
- Journal
- Align yourself
- Exercise
- Stretch
- Turn off notifications
- Organize
- Plan your days
- Plan your weeks
- Plan your months
- Clean
- Do a task at a time consciously
- Listen to podcasts
- Express gratitude
- Read
- Stay hydrated
- Watch inspiring videos
- Read inspiring quotes
- Create a beautiful environment
- Leave your phone during work
- Repeat affirmations
- Show love
- Sun gaze
- Ground yourself
- Stay true to yourself
- Say thank you to everyone
- Keep your back straight
- Eat healthy
- Network
- Meet new people
- Set short term goals
- Set mid term goals
- Set long term goals
- Donate to others in need
- Think positive thoughts
- Find balance
- Always believe
- Ignore the in-harmonious
- Visualize
- Ask for help
- Seek guidance
- Budget
- Practice communication
- Be kind
- Stay organized
- Help others in need
- Reflect
- Maintain a morning routine
- Consult a mentor or coach
- Work smarter
- Laugh
- Dance and sing

Self-Concept / Higher-Self

Date: _____

What are the qualities associated with your higher self?

What are the behaviors associated with your higher self?

What are the feelings associated with your higher self?

How can I visualize the embodiment of your higher self?

I embrace and obtain the same activities, habits, and qualities associated with my higher self. I no longer associate my future with my past. I am now reborn. I declare that I am now fully committed to being this person for the rest of my life.

Opposites Attract

Typically, inner resistance is triggered by uncertainty, doubt, fear, and judgment. In order to overcome this internal resistance, you must feel thoughts of an opposite nature and claim the ones that resonate most deeply and feel most empowering.

You cannot force yourself to stop thinking a thought. What you can do is direct your attention to another thought. Focus on empowering thoughts rather than limiting thoughts, and your limiting thoughts will begin to fade from your awareness. For example, in the past, one could desire to speak publicly, yet he encountered internal resistance that prevented him from doing so. He believed the limiting thought of: "I needed to know all the answers to every question before expressing my perspectives." He worked on it and discovered that fear and judgment were the root causes of this thought and internal resistance.

He took a step back and considered the opposites. He first saw a possibility that rather than being in a state where he needed to know all the answers, he could be in a state where he did know all the answers. There was not much resonance there. Then, he discovered and claimed the opposite thought, and it resonated most deeply with him. The thought was: "I do not need to know all the answers!" At that moment, everything changed as he transcended the barrier of resistance. By engaging in a little thought work, the internal resistance cleared, and his desire had the space to activate fully. As you learn to identify the source of internal resistance, you, too, will discover that the resistance is just temporary. Claim the opposite of the internal barrier, and imagine you possess the opposite of that which you are currently lacking.

Opposites Attract

RESISTANCE	IDENTIFY AND RELEASE THE CAUSE	OPPOSITE

I polarize in consciousness to the desired state. My natural state of consciousness is one of confidence, faith, conviction, love, and presence of mind.

For-Giving

Forgiveness is a critical aspect to note when manifesting. Forgiving others and forgiving self. Forgiving is necessary for healing and releasing what no longer serves you. If you have something deep within you that is bothering you, such as a grudge, resentment, or condemnation of any sort, it will be holding you back from expressing your higher self and manifesting the life you desire.

Forgive others by realizing their innocence. Everyone, including you, has been indoctrinated into a belief system that we did not choose. Look past one's beliefs and realize that deep down, they are innocent loving awareness. There is an I AM within all of us that is unconditioned and forgives and accepts us all, and the I AM within me is the same as the I AM within you.

If you constantly dwell on your past faults or someone wronging you, you will manifest dis-ease. You will begin viewing yourself as a victim in certain situations, which will inevitably obstruct your growth. While forgiving others and oneself is sometimes effortless for some and incredibly difficult for others, you will remain in an in-harmonious state unless you learn to forgive and let go.

You are far beyond a recollection of memories from the past. You are an Infinite Creator. Surrender and let go of what no longer serves you by choosing now to create what will. By letting go of control and surrendering, you will be able to forgive, accept, and transcend. On the next page, you will either choose circumstances to forgive yourself or circumstances to forgive others. You are required to write down why you forgive yourself or others, and visualize yourself accomplishing the act.

For-Giving

I FORGIVE...	WHY?

I understand. I accept. I forgive. I surrender. I let go. I transcend.
I forgive myself. I forgive others.
I AM innocent.

How To Use

A barcode is located on the back of this planner. After scanning the barcode with your smartphone, you can access the Manifestation Planner Tutorial, which includes a video with all of the necessary information, as well as step-by-step guidance for properly filling out this planner. Additionally, the back of this planner contains pre-filled pages that you can use as examples.

It is best to make this a habit; just as you wake up in the morning and brush your teeth without thinking about doing so, you can program your subconscious mind to wake up and make utilizing this planner a part of your habitual routine.

If you want to be effective and productive, you should be aware of what you are doing daily. Your days should be monotonous while incorporating variety and free time. I encourage you to wake up at the same time every morning and sleep at the same time every night. Have a committed morning and nightly routine. The more organized your days are, the greater you will know what the day will bring. You will dissolve uncertainty, and your subconscious mind will make your routines effortless.

You will enter a state of presence, trust, and flow due to obtaining a strong knowingness for the day. This flow state will assist you in overcoming any doubts, tension, procrastination, and worries. Most importantly, you will develop the necessary trust and belief in yourself. Before we explain the following pages, I must honor you. I honor you for embracing your limitless potential in your commitment to being your higher self and manifesting the life of your dreams. You are the one who is going to change it all.

Monthly, Weekly, & Daily Planner

This planner will provide you with monthly, weekly, and daily planning. In addition to planning your months, weeks, and days, you will be manifesting your heart's desires. Monthly and weekly manifestations are recommended, as some things do not materialize overnight. I encourage rewriting your weekly or monthly goals and aims as manifestations for the presented daily manifestation box, unless you have something specific you desire to manifest for that day.

Start on a Monday so your week can be organized and smooth. Write your manifestations and affirmations in the present tense, asserting them here and now. Use I AM, or I HAVE. Do not use I need, or I want because they do not exist now. Align yourself with your long-term vision, and your short-term goals and desires will be aligned accordingly. Be intentional and purposeful, and, of course, believe everything you write.

You will then be directed to a visualization box. Here, imagine yourself having your desire. Write down what you imagined, and include your emotions and feelings. Sit on a couch with your back straight, and take deep and slow breaths. You will enter an alpha-theta brain wave state, which is the state where transformation regularly occurs as your subconscious gets impressed with ease.

After visualization, you may open your eyes and see nothing has changed, but remember that what you see now is solely your previous state of consciousness objectified. Continue walking by faith, not by sight. Your final step is to acknowledge and claim your manifestation as received with an affirmation.

Daily Reflection

Once the daily planner is complete, you will be presented with a daily reflection. When reflecting, ensure you do not dwell on the negatives of the day. If it was an undesirable day, observe it for what it is and transcend it by learning from it. If a circumstance were to produce a limiting belief, revise your day by imagining and feeling it to have gone the way you desired it to go before bed.

Reflecting on your days is essential for coming to new realizations and evolving into higher states of consciousness, and it gets rid of all manifestation blocks. You will be asked: "What emotions did I feel?" Every day, we feel emotions. Whether joyful, sad, happy, or frustrated, you want to document it. Then, you will be required to describe what triggered that particular emotion.

Following that, you will record your daily accomplishments. When asked about your accomplishments, include anything as little as making your bed in the morning to going for a walk. Proceeding, you will remind yourself who you are with the following question: (Who am I? Really?) This question is meant to align with your higher self.

The next question is about learning. Without learning, you will be unable to realize your vision progressively. Learning lessons from temporary defeats, learning from people who are manifesting the same desire you wish to manifest, learning a new technique, or even learning a new way of being. We constantly learn, and with constant learning comes a constant evolution and expansion of our awareness. Your last question, "How can I improve tomorrow?" will conclude your daily reflection.

Weekly Reflection

Each week, you will come across a weekly reflection. You will be asked where you are now and what your goals and aims are next week in regard to the following matters: Physical, Mental, Spiritual, and Financial.

Afterward, you will be prompted to write your accomplishments for the week, including what you've learned and what you're grateful for. You will then be prompted to the question: What affirmations did I actualize this week? Here, you want to list your affirmations and how you expressed them. An example would be: "I am healthy is an affirmation I expressed by eating healthy foods all week."

You would then come across a prompt asking you to further realize your vision. What is further realizing your vision? This is the how of manifesting. When you have a thought or an idea, the way you manifest it is by realizing the vision to completion. It is essentially the ideas or steps you must take to manifest it. Don't think you NEED to do anything, for by expressing yourself as the person who has already realized the vision, the vision gets realized automatically. As you dwell in the realization of your vision, you begin expanding your awareness and aligning with the frequency of your desire, and as a result, opportunities to get you there will begin to present themselves automatically. Don't worry about how it will happen, just know it will happen, someway, somehow, for it's already yours. To assist you with how you will manifest your desire, make a list of the hunches you've received from your inner voice, what you feel your next steps are, the opportunities or ideas that came to you, and what has recently inspired you.

Monthly Alignment Tracker

Every month, you will have an alignment tracker. Complete this section as you go, and keep track of your days by checking the box as you complete your morning ritual. Your morning ritual is what you do when you first wake up, and it is the basis for your entire day. For ideas on what you would like your morning ritual to include, you can reflect on the qualities and behaviors associated with your higher self and implement them accordingly.

You will be required to write your morning ritual, visualize it, and affirm it. Before you sleep every night, I encourage you to visualize yourself successfully accomplishing your morning ritual. This will impress your subconscious mind and make it more effortless for you in the morning. Commit to your morning ritual until it becomes an automatic expression, meaning that you wake up and perform your morning ritual with little to no conscious effort. Committing to morning rituals will train your willpower and cause an ideal state of mind, one that brings out the feelings of your wishes being fulfilled. Accomplishing your morning routine will also aid you in focusing on upcoming tasks, managing your time, eliminating uncertainty, and increasing productivity.

Additionally, you will have three sections: habits to unlearn, habits to improve, and new habits to master. By identifying the habits that no longer serve you, you can replace them with those harmonious with your vision. This will result in you effortlessly attracting and realizing additional desires. As we continue reconditioning our state of consciousness, we evolve, our self-concept and self-image evolve, and our daily habits, behaviors, activities, and desires evolve.

Monthly Reflection

After completing the month, you will be required to write your top 10 achievements. By writing down your achievements, you will be able to connect the dots by being able to reflect and realize how you got to where you are now. Essentially, you will connect the dots backward from your previous achievements to here and now.

Be grateful for your small accomplishments, and celebrate your month in gratitude. You will be asked what you learned, alongside what obstacles you faced and overcame. Following this, you have the opportunity to revise any experience from the past that may not have gone the way you desired it to go.

When asked, "How could you revise a specific scenario?" Visualize an experience that you would have desired to go differently and imagine it to have gone the way you desired it to go.

The Revision Technique by Neville Goddard is the ultimate technique for abolishing any in-harmonious limiting beliefs embedded within. If there was a time in history when you were impressed by such a limiting belief, imagine it and revise it scene by scene to how you would have wanted it to occur in your imagination.

Do this until it seems so real that you feel you have experienced your revised day. Revising the past alters the future by substituting the past scenario for an ideal one, modifying your belief system to conform to your ideal. This works because the subconscious mind does not know the difference between what is real and what is not, as it goes based on thought and feeling.

Monthly Reflection

Everything is possible in an ideal belief system. "I'm not good enough" is frequently triggered by a past scenario where someone has told you that or a time in the past when you felt worthless. This limiting belief would simply cease to exist if the outcome of your experience was ideal due to the in-harmonious circumstance ceasing to exist.

Why do you think that the typical people who believe they always succeed continue to succeed? Those who believe they always fail, fail? Because those who have succeeded have developed a belief that if they succeed in one thing, they succeed in anything. Their failures do not matter, as they know their destination. Their ideal state of mind is one of "Anything is possible," whereas those who are victims of failure develop a belief that they will continue to fail based on prior experiences and scenarios. Therefore, revising one scenario could lead to a million different possibilities. All you must do is trust in your imagination to do the work.

Following the revision, you will be asked: "Where has your energy mostly been last month?" Are you protecting your energy, or are you trying to please others? To conclude your monthly reflection, you will be asked, how can you improve next month? Write this out in the present tense and use I AM.

Thank you for becoming a part of this community. I AM extremely grateful for you and excited for your quantum leap. I honor you for your alignment, your faith, your being, your work ethic, your love, your compassion, your capability to manifest anything and everything into your life, and being you. Let us create miracles.

It *will* happen in ways you can't possibly imagine.

- Dolores Cannon

Tips & Tricks For Manifesting

Detach yourself from the outcome. Stop trying to force things. Know that someway, somehow, your desire will manifest. Walk by faith, not by sight. Perceive all your experiences as circumstances meant for you to realize your vision, and realize that everything is happening for you, not to you.

Don't worry about when or how something will manifest. The when is an illusion, and the how is not for you to know. Express gratitude for what is already yours. Focusing on worrying about how things will happen will only express a lack of not having it. Make the shift from force to flow by surrendering and trusting.

Stay true to yourself. What you write is what you will do. Train your willpower accordingly, for if you begin being dishonest with yourself, you will lose trust in yourself, others, and ultimately your future. Alongside, you will weaken your willpower and lose faith. Integrity will lead you to trust yourself, strengthen your willpower, improve your reputation, and give you a greater sense of purpose.

Listen to the hunches of your inner voice. Listen to your heart's desires. Listen to what inspires you. Trust that your inner voice is guiding you to your heart, and trust that your heart will provide you with the necessary steps to realize your vision to completion. Commit to doing the right thing, and you will live a successful life.

Tips & Tricks For Manifesting

When in doubt, worry, or fear, do nothing. Your smartest decisions and your greatest actions are always those made in positive states. When inspired - in spirit - with your vision, you will create from love. This love will keep you in a state of flow, which will make your journey far more rewarding than your destination.

Assume and expect the best-case scenario. Neville Goddard says, "Assumptions harden into fact." What you assume will happen will happen. You dictate your outcome. Assuming should be done with the least amount of effort possible. By simply assuming, you are detached from the when and the how, and you release all worry.

Be Conscious and Present. Focus on now and whatever now brings. The everlasting eternal now is the only thing we will ever have, and it is only what is done now that counts. Focusing too much on the future can cause anxiety, while focusing on the past will merely prevent you from entering a new state of consciousness. Your desire exists here, now. It is simply waiting to be manifested.

Feel it. Feel the feeling of your desire granted. Make it your natural feeling. Do it habitually. Be grateful for what you have now and for what is to come. Declare it by asserting, "I AM! I AM! I AM THAT I AM!" Claim the awareness of being that which you desire to be until you have been taken over by undoubted certainty.

Monthly Planner

Month:

	Monday	Tuesday	Wednesday
Priorities			
Habits			
Intentions			

Monthly Manifestation	Visualization	Affirmation

Monthly Planner

Month:

Thursday	Friday	Saturday	Sunday

Notes

Alignment Tracker

Month:

Monday	Tuesday	Wednesday	Thursday	Friday	Saturday	Sunday

Morning Routine:

Visualization:

Affirmation:

Alignment Tracker

Month:

How do you feel going into next month?

What are the habits, activities, and behaviors to unlearn?

What are the habits, activities, and behaviors to improve on?

What are the new habits, activities, and behaviors to master?

I choose to live with integrity, to always be true to my values and beliefs. I am committed to being who I desire to be, who I say I am. I am striving to continuously learn and grow, and to make a positive impact in the world. I am in control.

Weekly Planner

Date:

Manifestation

Visualization

Affirmation

Schedule

Monday

Tuesday

Wednesday

Thursday

Friday

Saturday

Sunday

Priorities	To Do

It's already yours.

-Universe

Daily Planner

M T W T F S S

Date:

Manifestation

Schedule

6:00	
7:00	
8:00	
9:00	
10:00	
11:00	
12:00	
1:00	
2:00	
3:00	
4:00	
5:00	
6:00	
7:00	
8:00	
9:00	

Visualization

Affirmation

Today, I am grateful for...	Inspired Actions & Priorities	Reminders - To Do

Daily Reflection

Mood:

What emotion(s) did I feel?

What caused the emotion(s)?

What were my accomplishments?

Who am I? Really?

What did I learn today?

How can I improve tomorrow?

Daily Planner

M T W T F S S

Date:

Manifestation

Visualization

Affirmation

Schedule

6:00	
7:00	
8:00	
9:00	
10:00	
11:00	
12:00	
1:00	
2:00	
3:00	
4:00	
5:00	
6:00	
7:00	
8:00	
9:00	

Today, I am grateful for...	Inspired Actions & Priorities	Reminders – To Do

Daily Reflection

Mood:

What emotion(s) did I feel?

What caused the emotion(s)?

What were my accomplishments?

Who am I? Really?

What did I learn today?

How can I improve tomorrow?

Daily Planner

M T W T F S S

Date: 08/31/24

Manifestation

Schedule

6:00	Wake up, workout
7:00	
8:00	
9:00	
10:00	
11:00	
12:00	
1:00	
2:00	
3:00	
4:00	
5:00	
6:00	
7:00	
8:00	
9:00	

Visualization

Affirmation

Today, I am grateful for...	Inspired Actions & Priorities	Reminders – To Do

Daily Reflection

Mood:

What emotion(s) did I feel?

What caused the emotion(s)?

What were my accomplishments?

Who am I? Really?

What did I learn today?

How can I improve tomorrow?

Daily Planner

M T W T F S S

Date:

Manifestation

Schedule

6:00	
7:00	
8:00	
9:00	
10:00	

Visualization

11:00	
12:00	
1:00	
2:00	
3:00	

Affirmation

4:00	
5:00	
6:00	
7:00	
8:00	
9:00	

Today, I am grateful for...	Inspired Actions & Priorities	Reminders - To Do

Daily Reflection

Mood:

What emotion(s) did I feel?

What caused the emotion(s)?

What were my accomplishments?

Who am I? Really?

What did I learn today?

How can I improve tomorrow?

Daily Planner

M T W T F S S

Date:

Manifestation

Visualization

Affirmation

Schedule

6:00	
7:00	
8:00	
9:00	
10:00	
11:00	
12:00	
1:00	
2:00	
3:00	
4:00	
5:00	
6:00	
7:00	
8:00	
9:00	

Today, I am grateful for...	Inspired Actions & Priorities	Reminders - To Do

Daily Reflection

Mood:

What emotion(s) did I feel?

What caused the emotion(s)?

What were my accomplishments?

Who am I? Really?

What did I learn today?

How can I improve tomorrow?

Daily Planner

M T W T F S S

Date:

Manifestation

Schedule

6:00	
7:00	
8:00	
9:00	
10:00	
11:00	
12:00	
1:00	
2:00	
3:00	
4:00	
5:00	
6:00	
7:00	
8:00	
9:00	

Visualization

Affirmation

Today, I am grateful for...	Inspired Actions & Priorities	Reminders – To Do

Daily Reflection

Mood:

What emotion(s) did I feel?

What caused the emotion(s)?

What were my accomplishments?

Who am I? Really?

What did I learn today?

How can I improve tomorrow?

Daily Planner

M T W T F S S

Date:

Manifestation

Schedule

6:00	
7:00	
8:00	
9:00	
10:00	
11:00	
12:00	
1:00	
2:00	
3:00	
4:00	
5:00	
6:00	
7:00	
8:00	
9:00	

Visualization

Affirmation

Today, I am grateful for...	Inspired Actions & Priorities	Reminders - To Do

Daily Reflection

Mood:

What emotion(s) did I feel?

What caused the emotion(s)?

What were my accomplishments?

Who am I? Really?

What did I learn today?

How can I improve tomorrow?

Weekly Reflection

Date:

Where Am I Now?

Physical	Mental	Spiritual	Financial

Where Am I Going Next Week?

Physical	Mental	Spiritual	Financial

Weekly Reflection

Date:

What were my biggest accomplishments this week?

What lessons did I learn this week?

What have I been most grateful for this week?

What affirmations did I actualize this week?

How can I further realize my vision?

Weekly Planner

Date:

Manifestation

Visualization

Affirmation

Schedule

Monday
Tuesday
Wednesday
Thursday
Friday
Saturday
Sunday

Priorities	To Do

Weekly Mantra

1111

I am innocent, divine, loving awareness. I am at peace with what was, in love with is, and inspired with what will be. I leave all my worries to the God of my understanding. I look at obstacles as opportunities to grow, and I stay true to myself. As time goes on, my awareness gradually expands. I learn new things, and I meet new people. It seems as if the Universe is giving me all that I need to manifest my desires. The Universe is conspiring to make it all happen for me. I assume it as done. It's already mine. I walk confidently, knowing who I am, and knowing my destination is inevitable.

Daily Planner

M T W T F S S

Date:

Manifestation

Schedule

6:00	
7:00	
8:00	
9:00	
10:00	

Visualization

11:00	
12:00	
1:00	
2:00	
3:00	

Affirmation

4:00	
5:00	
6:00	
7:00	
8:00	
9:00	

Today, I am grateful for...	Inspired Actions & Priorities	Reminders – To Do

Daily Reflection

Mood:

What emotion(s) did I feel?

What caused the emotion(s)?

What were my accomplishments?

Who am I? Really?

What did I learn today?

How can I improve tomorrow?

Daily Planner

M T W T F S S

Date:

Manifestation

Schedule

6:00	
7:00	
8:00	
9:00	
10:00	
11:00	
12:00	
1:00	
2:00	
3:00	
4:00	
5:00	
6:00	
7:00	
8:00	
9:00	

Visualization

Affirmation

Today, I am grateful for...	Inspired Actions & Priorities	Reminders – To Do

Daily Reflection

Mood:

What emotion(s) did I feel?

What caused the emotion(s)?

What were my accomplishments?

Who am I? Really?

What did I learn today?

How can I improve tomorrow?

Daily Planner

M T W T F S S

Date:

Manifestation

Schedule

6:00	
7:00	
8:00	
9:00	
10:00	
11:00	
12:00	
1:00	
2:00	
3:00	
4:00	
5:00	
6:00	
7:00	
8:00	
9:00	

Visualization

Affirmation

Today, I am grateful for...	Inspired Actions & Priorities	Reminders - To Do

Daily Reflection

Mood:

What emotion(s) did I feel?

What caused the emotion(s)?

What were my accomplishments?

Who am I? Really?

What did I learn today?

How can I improve tomorrow?

Daily Planner

M T W T F S S

Date:

Manifestation

Schedule

6:00	
7:00	
8:00	
9:00	
10:00	
11:00	
12:00	
1:00	
2:00	
3:00	
4:00	
5:00	
6:00	
7:00	
8:00	
9:00	

Visualization

Affirmation

Today, I am grateful for...	Inspired Actions & Priorities	Reminders – To Do

Daily Reflection

Mood:

What emotion(s) did I feel?

What caused the emotion(s)?

What were my accomplishments?

Who am I? Really?

What did I learn today?

How can I improve tomorrow?

Daily Planner

M T W T F S S

Date:

Manifestation

Visualization

Affirmation

Schedule

6:00	
7:00	
8:00	
9:00	
10:00	
11:00	
12:00	
1:00	
2:00	
3:00	
4:00	
5:00	
6:00	
7:00	
8:00	
9:00	

Today, I am grateful for...	Inspired Actions & Priorities	Reminders – To Do

Daily Reflection

Mood:

What emotion(s) did I feel?

What caused the emotion(s)?

What were my accomplishments?

Who am I? Really?

What did I learn today?

How can I improve tomorrow?

Daily Planner

M T W T F S S

Date:

Manifestation

Visualization

Affirmation

Schedule

6:00	
7:00	
8:00	
9:00	
10:00	
11:00	
12:00	
1:00	
2:00	
3:00	
4:00	
5:00	
6:00	
7:00	
8:00	
9:00	

Today, I am grateful for...	Inspired Actions & Priorities	Reminders - To Do

Daily Reflection

Mood:

What emotion(s) did I feel?

What caused the emotion(s)?

What were my accomplishments?

Who am I? Really?

What did I learn today?

How can I improve tomorrow?

Daily Planner

M T W T F S S

Date:

Manifestation

Schedule

6:00	
7:00	
8:00	
9:00	
10:00	

Visualization

11:00	
12:00	
1:00	
2:00	
3:00	
4:00	

Affirmation

5:00	
6:00	
7:00	
8:00	
9:00	

Today, I am grateful for...	Inspired Actions & Priorities	Reminders - To Do

Daily Reflection

Mood:

What emotion(s) did I feel?

What caused the emotion(s)?

What were my accomplishments?

Who am I? Really?

What did I learn today?

How can I improve tomorrow?

Weekly Reflection

Date:

Where Am I Now?

Physical	Mental	Spiritual	Financial

Where Am I Going Next Week?

Physical	Mental	Spiritual	Financial

Weekly Reflection

Date:

Where Am I Now?

Physical	Mental	Spiritual	Financial

Where Am I Going Next Week?

Physical	Mental	Spiritual	Financial

Weekly Reflection

Date:

What were my biggest accomplishments this week?

What lessons did I learn this week?

What have I been most grateful for this week?

What affirmations did I actualize this week?

How can I further realize my vision?

Weekly Planner

Date:

Manifestation

Schedule

Monday
Tuesday
Wednesday
Thursday
Friday
Saturday
Sunday

Visualization

Affirmation

Priorities	To Do

Weekly Mantra

444

I can feel it. I can feel the feeling of my wishes fulfilled. I know it is all happening for me. Even when life tells me no, I persist with faith. I stay loyal to my vision, and I won't stop until it manifests. My imagination creates my reality. I rely on the evidence of what I imagine rather than the evidence of my circumstances. I imagine my life the exact way I desire it to be and assume that I am living it. I assume that I already have what I desire. I assume that the Universe will pave the way to my heart's desires. I visualize my life the way I want it to be, and I watch it become. I am the creator.

Daily Planner

M T W T F S S

Date:

Manifestation

Visualization

Affirmation

Schedule	
6:00	
7:00	
8:00	
9:00	
10:00	
11:00	
12:00	
1:00	
2:00	
3:00	
4:00	
5:00	
6:00	
7:00	
8:00	
9:00	

Today, I am grateful for...	Inspired Actions & Priorities	Reminders – To Do

Daily Reflection

Mood:

What emotion(s) did I feel?

What caused the emotion(s)?

What were my accomplishments?

Who am I? Really?

What did I learn today?

How can I improve tomorrow?

Daily Planner

M T W T F S S

Date:

Manifestation

Schedule

6:00	
7:00	
8:00	
9:00	
10:00	

Visualization

11:00	
12:00	
1:00	
2:00	
3:00	

Affirmation

4:00	
5:00	
6:00	
7:00	
8:00	
9:00	

Today, I am grateful for...	Inspired Actions & Priorities	Reminders – To Do

Daily Reflection

Mood:

What emotion(s) did I feel?

What caused the emotion(s)?

What were my accomplishments?

Who am I? Really?

What did I learn today?

How can I improve tomorrow?

Daily Planner

M T W T F S S

Date:

Manifestation

Visualization

Affirmation

Schedule

6:00	
7:00	
8:00	
9:00	
10:00	
11:00	
12:00	
1:00	
2:00	
3:00	
4:00	
5:00	
6:00	
7:00	
8:00	
9:00	

Today, I am grateful for...	Inspired Actions & Priorities	Reminders – To Do

Daily Reflection

Mood:

What emotion(s) did I feel?

What caused the emotion(s)?

What were my accomplishments?

Who am I? Really?

What did I learn today?

How can I improve tomorrow?

Daily Planner

M T W T F S S

Date:

Manifestation

Schedule

6:00	
7:00	
8:00	
9:00	
10:00	

Visualization

11:00	
12:00	
1:00	
2:00	
3:00	

Affirmation

4:00	
5:00	
6:00	
7:00	
8:00	
9:00	

Today, I am grateful for...	Inspired Actions & Priorities	Reminders - To Do

Daily Reflection

Mood:

What emotion(s) did I feel?

What caused the emotion(s)?

What were my accomplishments?

Who am I? Really?

What did I learn today?

How can I improve tomorrow?

Daily Planner

M T W T F S S

Date:

Manifestation

Schedule

6:00	
7:00	
8:00	
9:00	
10:00	
11:00	
12:00	
1:00	
2:00	
3:00	
4:00	
5:00	
6:00	
7:00	
8:00	
9:00	

Visualization

Affirmation

Today, I am grateful for...	Inspired Actions & Priorities	Reminders - To Do

Daily Reflection

Mood:

What emotion(s) did I feel?

What caused the emotion(s)?

What were my accomplishments?

Who am I? Really?

What did I learn today?

How can I improve tomorrow?

Daily Planner

M T W T F S S

Date:

Manifestation

Schedule

6:00	
7:00	
8:00	
9:00	
10:00	
11:00	
12:00	

Visualization

1:00	
2:00	
3:00	
4:00	

Affirmation

5:00	
6:00	
7:00	
8:00	
9:00	

Today, I am grateful for...	Inspired Actions & Priorities	Reminders - To Do

Daily Reflection

Mood:

What emotion(s) did I feel?

What caused the emotion(s)?

What were my accomplishments?

Who am I? Really?

What did I learn today?

How can I improve tomorrow?

Daily Planner

M T W T F S S

Date:

Manifestation

Visualization

Affirmation

Schedule

Time	
6:00	
7:00	
8:00	
9:00	
10:00	
11:00	
12:00	
1:00	
2:00	
3:00	
4:00	
5:00	
6:00	
7:00	
8:00	
9:00	

Today, I am grateful for...	Inspired Actions & Priorities	Reminders - To Do

Daily Reflection

Mood:

What emotion(s) did I feel?

What caused the emotion(s)?

What were my accomplishments?

Who am I? Really?

What did I learn today?

How can I improve tomorrow?

Weekly Reflection

Date:

Where Am I Now?

Physical	Mental	Spiritual	Financial

Where Am I Going Next Week?

Physical	Mental	Spiritual	Financial

Weekly Reflection

Date:

Where Am I Now?

Physical	Mental	Spiritual	Financial

Where Am I Going Next Week?

Physical	Mental	Spiritual	Financial

Weekly Reflection

Date:

What were my biggest accomplishments this week?

What lessons did I learn this week?

What have I been most grateful for this week?

What affirmations did I actualize this week?

How can I further realize my vision?

Weekly Planner

Date:

Manifestation

Visualization

Affirmation

Schedule

Monday	
Tuesday	
Wednesday	
Thursday	
Friday	
Saturday	
Sunday	

Priorities	To Do

Weekly Mantra

888

I have fun. I don't take life too seriously. I play the game of life with ease. I let love take its course and watch miracles manifest before my very eyes. I don't even have to try to manifest my desires. It happens naturally. Just by being who I am, I attract what I want. I am in vibrational harmony with my vision. All things good come shooting into my electromagnetic field. Abundance, Love, and Peace are my birthright. Even when things don't go my way, I don't worry. I flow through my life with love and let the Universe do the rest. I rest assured knowing that life happens for me to learn more about who I really am.

Daily Planner

M T W T F S S

Date:

Manifestation

Schedule

6:00	
7:00	
8:00	
9:00	
10:00	
11:00	
12:00	
1:00	
2:00	
3:00	
4:00	
5:00	
6:00	
7:00	
8:00	
9:00	

Visualization

Affirmation

Today, I am grateful for...	Inspired Actions & Priorities	Reminders – To Do

Daily Reflection

Mood:

What emotion(s) did I feel?

What caused the emotion(s)?

What were my accomplishments?

Who am I? Really?

What did I learn today?

How can I improve tomorrow?

Daily Planner

M T W T F S S

Date:

Manifestation

Schedule

6:00	
7:00	
8:00	
9:00	
10:00	
11:00	
12:00	
1:00	
2:00	
3:00	
4:00	
5:00	
6:00	
7:00	
8:00	
9:00	

Visualization

Affirmation

Today, I am grateful for...	Inspired Actions & Priorities	Reminders - To Do

Daily Reflection

Mood:

What emotion(s) did I feel?

What caused the emotion(s)?

What were my accomplishments?

Who am I? Really?

What did I learn today?

How can I improve tomorrow?

Daily Planner

M T W T F S S

Date:

Manifestation

Visualization

Affirmation

Schedule

6:00	
7:00	
8:00	
9:00	
10:00	
11:00	
12:00	
1:00	
2:00	
3:00	
4:00	
5:00	
6:00	
7:00	
8:00	
9:00	

Today, I am grateful for...	Inspired Actions & Priorities	Reminders - To Do

Daily Reflection

Mood:

What emotion(s) did I feel?

What caused the emotion(s)?

What were my accomplishments?

Who am I? Really?

What did I learn today?

How can I improve tomorrow?

Daily Planner

M T W T F S S

Date:

Manifestation

Schedule

6:00	
7:00	
8:00	
9:00	

Visualization

10:00	
11:00	
12:00	
1:00	
2:00	
3:00	

Affirmation

4:00	
5:00	
6:00	
7:00	
8:00	
9:00	

Today, I am grateful for...	Inspired Actions & Priorities	Reminders – To Do

Daily Reflection

Mood: _____

What emotion(s) did I feel?

What caused the emotion(s)?

What were my accomplishments?

Who am I? Really?

What did I learn today?

How can I improve tomorrow?

Daily Planner

M T W T F S S

Date:

Manifestation

Schedule

6:00	
7:00	
8:00	
9:00	
10:00	

Visualization

11:00	
12:00	
1:00	
2:00	
3:00	
4:00	

Affirmation

5:00	
6:00	
7:00	
8:00	
9:00	

Today, I am grateful for...	Inspired Actions & Priorities	Reminders – To Do

Daily Reflection

Mood:

What emotion(s) did I feel?

What caused the emotion(s)?

What were my accomplishments?

Who am I? Really?

What did I learn today?

How can I improve tomorrow?

Daily Planner

M T W T F S S

Date:

Manifestation

Schedule

6:00	
7:00	
8:00	
9:00	
10:00	

Visualization

11:00	
12:00	
1:00	
2:00	
3:00	

Affirmation

4:00	
5:00	
6:00	
7:00	
8:00	
9:00	

Today, I am grateful for...	Inspired Actions & Priorities	Reminders – To Do

Daily Reflection

Mood:

What emotion(s) did I feel?

What caused the emotion(s)?

What were my accomplishments?

Who am I? Really?

What did I learn today?

How can I improve tomorrow?

Daily Planner

M T W T F S S

Date:

Manifestation

Visualization

Affirmation

Schedule

6:00	
7:00	
8:00	
9:00	
10:00	
11:00	
12:00	
1:00	
2:00	
3:00	
4:00	
5:00	
6:00	
7:00	
8:00	
9:00	

Today, I am grateful for...	Inspired Actions & Priorities	Reminders – To Do

Daily Reflection

Mood:

What emotion(s) did I feel?

What caused the emotion(s)?

What were my accomplishments?

Who am I? Really?

What did I learn today?

How can I improve tomorrow?

Weekly Reflection

Date:

Where Am I Now?

Physical	Mental	Spiritual	Financial

Where Am I Going Next Week?

Physical	Mental	Spiritual	Financial

Weekly Reflection

Date:

What were my biggest accomplishments this week?

What lessons did I learn this week?

What have I been most grateful for this week?

What affirmations did I actualize this week?

How can I further realize my vision?

Monthly Reflection

Month:

Top 10 Achievements

1. _____
2. _____
3. _____
4. _____
5. _____

6. _____
7. _____
8. _____
9. _____
10. _____

What have I been most grateful for this month?

What did I learn this month?

What obstacles did I face/overcome this month?

Monthly Reflection

Month:

Can I revise a specific scenario?

Where has my energy mostly been this month?

How can I improve for next month?

Monthly Planner

Month:

	Monday	Tuesday	Wednesday
Priorities			
Habits			
Intentions			

Monthly Manifestation	Visualization	Affirmation

Monthly Planner

Month:

Thursday	Friday	Saturday	Sunday

Notes

Alignment Tracker

Month:

Monday	Tuesday	Wednesday	Thursday	Friday	Saturday	Sunday

Morning Routine:

Visualization:

Affirmation:

Alignment Tracker

Month:

How do you feel going into next month?

What are the habits, activities, and behaviors to unlearn?

What are the habits, activities, and behaviors to improve on?

What are the new habits, activities, and behaviors to master?

I acknowledge and embrace the obstacles in my path as opportunities for growth. I trust in my strength and ability to overcome any challenge. I rise above limiting beliefs and embrace my unlimited potential. I am committed to expanding my consciousness and tapping into the wisdom within. I embrace my authentic self and live in alignment with my values. I am the one I desire to be.

Weekly Planner

Date:

Manifestation

Visualization

Affirmation

Schedule

Monday	
Tuesday	
Wednesday	
Thursday	
Friday	
Saturday	
Sunday	

Priorities	To Do

Weekly Mantra

777

I am aware of being all that I desire. I am aware of having all that I desire. I awaken to my own power and potential. I cultivate awareness and embrace my inner wisdom. I let go of limiting beliefs and embrace infinite possibilities. I focus on the present moment and live with intention. I am open to growth and new experiences. I trust the journey and allow myself to flow with ease and grace. I am fully present, fully conscious and fully alive in each moment. There is nothing I need, for all that I need exists within me. I already have all that I need. I tap into the place of infinite supply within me, and I watch as infinite supply begins to manifest for me.

Daily Planner

M T W T F S S

Date:

Manifestation

Schedule

6:00	
7:00	
8:00	
9:00	
10:00	

Visualization

11:00	
12:00	
1:00	
2:00	
3:00	

Affirmation

4:00	
5:00	
6:00	
7:00	
8:00	
9:00	

Today, I am grateful for...	Inspired Actions & Priorities	Reminders - To Do

Daily Reflection

Mood:

What emotion(s) did I feel?

What caused the emotion(s)?

What were my accomplishments?

Who am I? Really?

What did I learn today?

How can I improve tomorrow?

Daily Planner

M T W T F S S

Date:

Manifestation

Visualization

Affirmation

Schedule

6:00	
7:00	
8:00	
9:00	
10:00	
11:00	
12:00	
1:00	
2:00	
3:00	
4:00	
5:00	
6:00	
7:00	
8:00	
9:00	

Today, I am grateful for...	Inspired Actions & Priorities	Reminders – To Do

Daily Reflection

Mood:

What emotion(s) did I feel?

What caused the emotion(s)?

What were my accomplishments?

Who am I? Really?

What did I learn today?

How can I improve tomorrow?

Daily Planner

M T W T F S S

Date:

Manifestation

Visualization

Affirmation

Schedule

6:00	
7:00	
8:00	
9:00	
10:00	
11:00	
12:00	
1:00	
2:00	
3:00	
4:00	
5:00	
6:00	
7:00	
8:00	
9:00	

Today, I am grateful for...	Inspired Actions & Priorities	Reminders – To Do

Daily Reflection

Mood:

What emotion(s) did I feel?

What caused the emotion(s)?

What were my accomplishments?

Who am I? Really?

What did I learn today?

How can I improve tomorrow?

Daily Planner

M T W T F S S

Date:

Manifestation

Schedule

6:00	
7:00	
8:00	
9:00	
10:00	

Visualization

11:00	
12:00	
1:00	
2:00	
3:00	

Affirmation

4:00	
5:00	
6:00	
7:00	
8:00	
9:00	

Today, I am grateful for...	Inspired Actions & Priorities	Reminders - To Do

Daily Reflection

Mood:

What emotion(s) did I feel?

What caused the emotion(s)?

What were my accomplishments?

Who am I? Really?

What did I learn today?

How can I improve tomorrow?

Daily Planner

M T W T F S S

Date:

Manifestation

Schedule

6:00	
7:00	
8:00	
9:00	
10:00	
11:00	
12:00	
1:00	
2:00	
3:00	
4:00	
5:00	
6:00	
7:00	
8:00	
9:00	

Visualization

Affirmation

Today, I am grateful for...	Inspired Actions & Priorities	Reminders - To Do

Daily Reflection

Mood:

What emotion(s) did I feel?

What caused the emotion(s)?

What were my accomplishments?

Who am I? Really?

What did I learn today?

How can I improve tomorrow?

Daily Planner

M T W T F S S

Date:

Manifestation

Visualization

Affirmation

Schedule

6:00	
7:00	
8:00	
9:00	
10:00	
11:00	
12:00	
1:00	
2:00	
3:00	
4:00	
5:00	
6:00	
7:00	
8:00	
9:00	

Today, I am grateful for...	Inspired Actions & Priorities	Reminders – To Do

Daily Reflection

Mood:

What emotion(s) did I feel?

What caused the emotion(s)?

What were my accomplishments?

Who am I? Really?

What did I learn today?

How can I improve tomorrow?

Daily Planner

M T W T F S S

Date:

Manifestation

Schedule

6:00	
7:00	
8:00	
9:00	
10:00	
11:00	
12:00	
1:00	
2:00	
3:00	
4:00	
5:00	
6:00	
7:00	
8:00	
9:00	

Visualization

Affirmation

Today, I am grateful for...	Inspired Actions & Priorities	Reminders – To Do

Daily Reflection

Mood:

What emotion(s) did I feel?

What caused the emotion(s)?

What were my accomplishments?

Who am I? Really?

What did I learn today?

How can I improve tomorrow?

Weekly Reflection

Date:

Where Am I Now?

Physical	Mental	Spiritual	Financial

Where Am I Going Next Week?

Physical	Mental	Spiritual	Financial

Weekly Reflection

Date:

What were my biggest accomplishments this week?

What lessons did I learn this week?

What have I been most grateful for this week?

What affirmations did I actualize this week?

How can I further realize my vision?

Weekly Planner

Date:

Manifestation

Visualization

Affirmation

Schedule

Monday

Tuesday

Wednesday

Thursday

Friday

Saturday

Sunday

Priorities	To Do

Weekly Mantra

888

I create the story of my life and I have the power to make it whatever I please. I can use the power of my awareness to look at things from a different perspective, thus changing the reality in which I live. I can use the power of my imagination to create a new life from a new perspective. I can view life the way I choose to. I realize I truly have no limitations, as I laugh at any doubts floating through my head. I know these doubts don't belong in my awareness, so I simply observe them with no attachment. As I continue to feel and claim faithful thoughts, my doubts fade away into the dust. I use my mind and body as tools, instead of being controlled by them. I create in the quantum field.

Daily Planner

M T W T F S S

Date:

Manifestation

Visualization

Affirmation

Schedule

6:00	
7:00	
8:00	
9:00	
10:00	
11:00	
12:00	
1:00	
2:00	
3:00	
4:00	
5:00	
6:00	
7:00	
8:00	
9:00	

Today, I am grateful for...	Inspired Actions & Priorities	Reminders – To Do

Daily Reflection

Mood:

What emotion(s) did I feel?

What caused the emotion(s)?

What were my accomplishments?

Who am I? Really?

What did I learn today?

How can I improve tomorrow?

Daily Planner

M T W T F S S

Date:

Manifestation

Visualization

Affirmation

Schedule

6:00	
7:00	
8:00	
9:00	
10:00	
11:00	
12:00	
1:00	
2:00	
3:00	
4:00	
5:00	
6:00	
7:00	
8:00	
9:00	

Today, I am grateful for...	Inspired Actions & Priorities	Reminders – To Do

Daily Reflection

Mood:

What emotion(s) did I feel?

What caused the emotion(s)?

What were my accomplishments?

Who am I? Really?

What did I learn today?

How can I improve tomorrow?

Daily Planner

M T W T F S S

Date:

Manifestation

Visualization

Affirmation

Schedule
6:00
7:00
8:00
9:00
10:00
11:00
12:00
1:00
2:00
3:00
4:00
5:00
6:00
7:00
8:00
9:00

Today, I am grateful for...	Inspired Actions & Priorities	Reminders – To Do

Daily Reflection

Mood:

What emotion(s) did I feel?

What caused the emotion(s)?

What were my accomplishments?

Who am I? Really?

What did I learn today?

How can I improve tomorrow?

Daily Planner

M T W T F S S

Date:

Manifestation

Visualization

Affirmation

Schedule

6:00	
7:00	
8:00	
9:00	
10:00	
11:00	
12:00	
1:00	
2:00	
3:00	
4:00	
5:00	
6:00	
7:00	
8:00	
9:00	

Today, I am grateful for...	Inspired Actions & Priorities	Reminders – To Do

Daily Reflection

Mood:

What emotion(s) did I feel?

What caused the emotion(s)?

What were my accomplishments?

Who am I? Really?

What did I learn today?

How can I improve tomorrow?

Daily Planner

M T W T F S S

Date:

Manifestation

Visualization

Affirmation

Schedule

6:00	
7:00	
8:00	
9:00	
10:00	
11:00	
12:00	
1:00	
2:00	
3:00	
4:00	
5:00	
6:00	
7:00	
8:00	
9:00	

Today, I am grateful for...	Inspired Actions & Priorities	Reminders - To Do

Daily Reflection

Mood:

What emotion(s) did I feel?

What caused the emotion(s)?

What were my accomplishments?

Who am I? Really?

What did I learn today?

How can I improve tomorrow?

Daily Planner

M T W T F S S

Date:

Manifestation

Schedule

6:00	
7:00	
8:00	
9:00	
10:00	

Visualization

11:00	
12:00	
1:00	
2:00	
3:00	
4:00	

Affirmation

5:00	
6:00	
7:00	
8:00	
9:00	

Today, I am grateful for...	Inspired Actions & Priorities	Reminders – To Do

Daily Reflection

Mood:

What emotion(s) did I feel?

What caused the emotion(s)?

What were my accomplishments?

Who am I? Really?

What did I learn today?

How can I improve tomorrow?

Daily Planner

M T W T F S S

Date:

Manifestation

Visualization

Affirmation

Schedule

6:00	
7:00	
8:00	
9:00	
10:00	
11:00	
12:00	
1:00	
2:00	
3:00	
4:00	
5:00	
6:00	
7:00	
8:00	
9:00	

Today, I am grateful for...	Inspired Actions & Priorities	Reminders – To Do

Daily Reflection

Mood:

What emotion(s) did I feel?

What caused the emotion(s)?

What were my accomplishments?

Who am I? Really?

What did I learn today?

How can I improve tomorrow?

Weekly Reflection

Date:

Where Am I Now?

Physical	Mental	Spiritual	Financial

Where Am I Going Next Week?

Physical	Mental	Spiritual	Financial

Weekly Reflection

Date: _____

What were my biggest accomplishments this week?

What lessons did I learn this week?

What have I been most grateful for this week?

What affirmations did I actualize this week?

How can I further realize my vision?

Weekly Planner

Date:

Manifestation

Visualization

Affirmation

Schedule

Monday

Tuesday

Wednesday

Thursday

Friday

Saturday

Sunday

Priorities	To Do

Weekly Mantra

999

I realize that my vision is meant for me, and me only. I realize that we are all here with a unique purpose, and that unique purpose is to fully express who we are through the medium of desire. When a desire comes my way, I realize that it is the Universe wanting to be expressed, so I express it. I know the difference between the desires of the outer world and the desires of my inner world. When a desire comes my way, I give thanks, for I know that it is already mine. I create in silence. I do not tell people my every move. I do what I do and let them see and confirm the change. I be the best version of myself and show up as that person with all who cross my path.

Daily Planner

M T W T F S S

Date:

Manifestation

Visualization

Affirmation

Schedule	
6:00	
7:00	
8:00	
9:00	
10:00	
11:00	
12:00	
1:00	
2:00	
3:00	
4:00	
5:00	
6:00	
7:00	
8:00	
9:00	

Today, I am grateful for...	Inspired Actions & Priorities	Reminders - To Do

Daily Reflection

Mood:

What emotion(s) did I feel?

What caused the emotion(s)?

What were my accomplishments?

Who am I? Really?

What did I learn today?

How can I improve tomorrow?

Daily Planner

M T W T F S S

Date:

Manifestation

Schedule

6:00	
7:00	
8:00	
9:00	
10:00	

Visualization

11:00	
12:00	
1:00	
2:00	
3:00	
4:00	

Affirmation

5:00	
6:00	
7:00	
8:00	
9:00	

Today, I am grateful for...	Inspired Actions & Priorities	Reminders - To Do

Daily Reflection

Mood:

What emotion(s) did I feel?

What caused the emotion(s)?

What were my accomplishments?

Who am I? Really?

What did I learn today?

How can I improve tomorrow?

Daily Planner

M T W T F S S

Date:

Manifestation

Schedule

6:00	
7:00	
8:00	
9:00	
10:00	

Visualization

11:00	
12:00	
1:00	
2:00	
3:00	

Affirmation

4:00	
5:00	
6:00	
7:00	
8:00	
9:00	

Today, I am grateful for...	Inspired Actions & Priorities	Reminders - To Do

Daily Reflection

Mood:

What emotion(s) did I feel?

What caused the emotion(s)?

What were my accomplishments?

Who am I? Really?

What did I learn today?

How can I improve tomorrow?

Daily Planner

M T W T F S S

Date:

Manifestation

Schedule

Time	
6:00	
7:00	
8:00	
9:00	
10:00	
11:00	
12:00	
1:00	
2:00	
3:00	
4:00	
5:00	
6:00	
7:00	
8:00	
9:00	

Visualization

Affirmation

Today, I am grateful for...	Inspired Actions & Priorities	Reminders - To Do

Daily Reflection

Mood:

What emotion(s) did I feel?

What caused the emotion(s)?

What were my accomplishments?

Who am I? Really?

What did I learn today?

How can I improve tomorrow?

Daily Planner

M T W T F S S

Date:

Manifestation

Visualization

Affirmation

Schedule	
6:00	
7:00	
8:00	
9:00	
10:00	
11:00	
12:00	
1:00	
2:00	
3:00	
4:00	
5:00	
6:00	
7:00	
8:00	
9:00	

Today, I am grateful for...	Inspired Actions & Priorities	Reminders – To Do

Daily Reflection

Mood:

What emotion(s) did I feel?

What caused the emotion(s)?

What were my accomplishments?

Who am I? Really?

What did I learn today?

How can I improve tomorrow?

Daily Planner

M T W T F S S

Date:

Manifestation

Visualization

Affirmation

Schedule

6:00	
7:00	
8:00	
9:00	
10:00	
11:00	
12:00	
1:00	
2:00	
3:00	
4:00	
5:00	
6:00	
7:00	
8:00	
9:00	

Today, I am grateful for...	Inspired Actions & Priorities	Reminders – To Do

Daily Reflection

Mood:

What emotion(s) did I feel?

What caused the emotion(s)?

What were my accomplishments?

Who am I? Really?

What did I learn today?

How can I improve tomorrow?

Daily Planner

M T W T F S S

Date:

Manifestation

Schedule

6:00	
7:00	
8:00	
9:00	
10:00	

Visualization

11:00	
12:00	
1:00	
2:00	
3:00	

Affirmation

4:00	
5:00	
6:00	
7:00	
8:00	
9:00	

Today, I am grateful for...	Inspired Actions & Priorities	Reminders - To Do

Daily Reflection

Mood:

What emotion(s) did I feel?

What caused the emotion(s)?

What were my accomplishments?

Who am I? Really?

What did I learn today?

How can I improve tomorrow?

Weekly Reflection

Date:

Where Am I Now?

Physical	Mental	Spiritual	Financial

Where Am I Going Next Week?

Physical	Mental	Spiritual	Financial

Weekly Reflection

Date:

What were my biggest accomplishments this week?

What lessons did I learn this week?

What have I been most grateful for this week?

What affirmations did I actualize this week?

How can I further realize my vision?

Weekly Planner

Date:

Manifestation

Visualization

Affirmation

Schedule

Monday

Tuesday

Wednesday

Thursday

Friday

Saturday

Sunday

Priorities	To Do

Weekly Mantra

111

My awareness of myself is with pure love. I love everything about myself, and that is how I continuously attract an abundance of even more love into my life. I don't stress. I realize that everything always works out no matter what. I know I have the free will to view anything I want through a different lens and perspective, so I choose to view negative experiences as opportunities to grow and stay true to who I am. I choose to take my attention away from things that don't matter. If it doesn't align with my vision, I don't give it my energy. I know where energy goes, energy grows. I choose to protect my energy.

Daily Planner

M T W T F S S

Date:

Manifestation

Visualization

Affirmation

Schedule

6:00	
7:00	
8:00	
9:00	
10:00	
11:00	
12:00	
1:00	
2:00	
3:00	
4:00	
5:00	
6:00	
7:00	
8:00	
9:00	

Today, I am grateful for...	Inspired Actions & Priorities	Reminders – To Do

Daily Reflection

Mood:

What emotion(s) did I feel?

What caused the emotion(s)?

What were my accomplishments?

Who am I? Really?

What did I learn today?

How can I improve tomorrow?

Daily Planner

M T W T F S S

Date:

Manifestation

Schedule

6:00	
7:00	
8:00	
9:00	
10:00	
11:00	
12:00	
1:00	
2:00	
3:00	
4:00	
5:00	
6:00	
7:00	
8:00	
9:00	

Visualization

Affirmation

Today, I am grateful for...	Inspired Actions & Priorities	Reminders - To Do

Daily Reflection

Mood:

What emotion(s) did I feel?

What caused the emotion(s)?

What were my accomplishments?

Who am I? Really?

What did I learn today?

How can I improve tomorrow?

Daily Planner

M T W T F S S

Date:

Manifestation

Visualization

Affirmation

Schedule

6:00	
7:00	
8:00	
9:00	
10:00	
11:00	
12:00	
1:00	
2:00	
3:00	
4:00	
5:00	
6:00	
7:00	
8:00	
9:00	

Today, I am grateful for...	Inspired Actions & Priorities	Reminders – To Do

Daily Reflection

Mood:

What emotion(s) did I feel?

What caused the emotion(s)?

What were my accomplishments?

Who am I? Really?

What did I learn today?

How can I improve tomorrow?

Daily Planner

M T W T F S S

Date:

Manifestation

Visualization

Affirmation

Schedule

6:00	
7:00	
8:00	
9:00	
10:00	
11:00	
12:00	
1:00	
2:00	
3:00	
4:00	
5:00	
6:00	
7:00	
8:00	
9:00	

Today, I am grateful for...	Inspired Actions & Priorities	Reminders – To Do

Daily Reflection

Mood:

What emotion(s) did I feel?

What caused the emotion(s)?

What were my accomplishments?

Who am I? Really?

What did I learn today?

How can I improve tomorrow?

Daily Planner

M T W T F S S

Date:

Manifestation

Schedule

6:00	
7:00	
8:00	
9:00	
10:00	
11:00	
12:00	
1:00	
2:00	
3:00	
4:00	
5:00	
6:00	
7:00	
8:00	
9:00	

Visualization

Affirmation

Today, I am grateful for...	Inspired Actions & Priorities	Reminders - To Do

Daily Reflection

Mood:

What emotion(s) did I feel?

What caused the emotion(s)?

What were my accomplishments?

Who am I? Really?

What did I learn today?

How can I improve tomorrow?

Daily Planner

M T W T F S S

Date:

Manifestation

Visualization

Affirmation

Schedule

6:00	
7:00	
8:00	
9:00	
10:00	
11:00	
12:00	
1:00	
2:00	
3:00	
4:00	
5:00	
6:00	
7:00	
8:00	
9:00	

Today, I am grateful for...	Inspired Actions & Priorities	Reminders - To Do

Daily Reflection

Mood:

What emotion(s) did I feel?

What caused the emotion(s)?

What were my accomplishments?

Who am I? Really?

What did I learn today?

How can I improve tomorrow?

Daily Planner

M T W T F S S

Date:

Manifestation

Visualization

Affirmation

Schedule	
6:00	
7:00	
8:00	
9:00	
10:00	
11:00	
12:00	
1:00	
2:00	
3:00	
4:00	
5:00	
6:00	
7:00	
8:00	
9:00	

Today, I am grateful for...	Inspired Actions & Priorities	Reminders - To Do

Daily Reflection

Mood:

What emotion(s) did I feel?

What caused the emotion(s)?

What were my accomplishments?

Who am I? Really?

What did I learn today?

How can I improve tomorrow?

Weekly Reflection   Date:

Where Am I Now?

Physical	Mental	Spiritual	Financial

Where Am I Going Next Week?

Physical	Mental	Spiritual	Financial

Weekly Reflection

Date:

What were my biggest accomplishments this week?

What lessons did I learn this week?

What have I been most grateful for this week?

What affirmations did I actualize this week?

How can I further realize my vision?

Monthly Reflection

Month:

Top 10 Achievements

1. _____
2. _____
3. _____
4. _____
5. _____

6. _____
7. _____
8. _____
9. _____
10. _____

What have I been most grateful for this month?

What did I learn this month?

What obstacles did I face/overcome this month?

Monthly Reflection

Month:

Can I revise a specific scenario?

Where has my energy mostly been this month?

How can I improve for next month?

Monthly Planner

Month:

	Monday	Tuesday	Wednesday
Priorities			
Habits			
Intentions			

Monthly Manifestation	Visualization	Affirmation

Monthly Planner

Month:

Thursday	Friday	Saturday	Sunday

Notes

Alignment Tracker

Month:

Monday	Tuesday	Wednesday	Thursday	Friday	Saturday	Sunday

Morning Routine:

Visualization:

Affirmation:

Alignment Tracker

Month:

How do you feel going into next month?

What are the habits, activities, and behaviors to unlearn?

What are the habits, activities, and behaviors to improve on?

What are the new habits, activities, and behaviors to master?

I nurture my mind, body and spirit every day. I align my thoughts, words and actions with my highest values. I surround myself with positivity and uplifting energies. I trust in my own journey and embrace my unique path to greatness. At this very moment, I give thanks.

Weekly Planner

Date:

Manifestation

Visualization

Affirmation

Schedule

Monday

Tuesday

Wednesday

Thursday

Friday

Saturday

Sunday

Priorities	To Do

Weekly Mantra

222

I make choices every single day. Today, I choose to be prosperous, abundant, healthy and loved. Today, I choose to be the energy I want to attract. I choose to treat others how I would want to be treated. Today, I choose love. I choose to love every little thing I do. I choose to love every person that walks across my path. Today, I choose to forgive myself, and others. I choose to release all doubts, limitations, and fears. Today, I choose faith. I know that I am safe in faith, and I know that I am safe in love.

Daily Planner

M T W T F S S

Date:

Manifestation

Schedule

6:00	
7:00	
8:00	
9:00	

Visualization

10:00	
11:00	
12:00	
1:00	
2:00	
3:00	

Affirmation

4:00	
5:00	
6:00	
7:00	
8:00	
9:00	

Today, I am grateful for...	Inspired Actions & Priorities	Reminders - To Do

Daily Reflection

Mood:

What emotion(s) did I feel?

What caused the emotion(s)?

What were my accomplishments?

Who am I? Really?

What did I learn today?

How can I improve tomorrow?

Daily Planner

M T W T F S S

Date:

Manifestation

Visualization

Affirmation

Schedule

6:00	
7:00	
8:00	
9:00	
10:00	
11:00	
12:00	
1:00	
2:00	
3:00	
4:00	
5:00	
6:00	
7:00	
8:00	
9:00	

Today, I am grateful for...	Inspired Actions & Priorities	Reminders – To Do

Daily Reflection

Mood:

What emotion(s) did I feel?

What caused the emotion(s)?

What were my accomplishments?

Who am I? Really?

What did I learn today?

How can I improve tomorrow?

Daily Planner

M T W T F S S

Date:

Manifestation

Schedule

6:00	
7:00	
8:00	
9:00	
10:00	
11:00	
12:00	
1:00	
2:00	
3:00	
4:00	
5:00	
6:00	
7:00	
8:00	
9:00	

Visualization

Affirmation

Today, I am grateful for...	Inspired Actions & Priorities	Reminders – To Do

Daily Reflection

Mood:

What emotion(s) did I feel?

What caused the emotion(s)?

What were my accomplishments?

Who am I? Really?

What did I learn today?

How can I improve tomorrow?

Daily Planner

M T W T F S S

Date:

Manifestation

Schedule

6:00	
7:00	
8:00	
9:00	
10:00	
11:00	
12:00	
1:00	
2:00	
3:00	
4:00	
5:00	
6:00	
7:00	
8:00	
9:00	

Visualization

Affirmation

Today, I am grateful for...	Inspired Actions & Priorities	Reminders - To Do

Daily Reflection

Mood:

What emotion(s) did I feel?

What caused the emotion(s)?

What were my accomplishments?

Who am I? Really?

What did I learn today?

How can I improve tomorrow?

Daily Planner

M T W T F S S

Date:

Manifestation

Visualization

Affirmation

Schedule

6:00	
7:00	
8:00	
9:00	
10:00	
11:00	
12:00	
1:00	
2:00	
3:00	
4:00	
5:00	
6:00	
7:00	
8:00	
9:00	

Today, I am grateful for...	Inspired Actions & Priorities	Reminders - To Do

Daily Reflection

Mood:

What emotion(s) did I feel?

What caused the emotion(s)?

What were my accomplishments?

Who am I? Really?

What did I learn today?

How can I improve tomorrow?

Daily Planner

M T W T F S S

Date:

Manifestation

Visualization

Affirmation

Schedule	
6:00	
7:00	
8:00	
9:00	
10:00	
11:00	
12:00	
1:00	
2:00	
3:00	
4:00	
5:00	
6:00	
7:00	
8:00	
9:00	

Today, I am grateful for...	Inspired Actions & Priorities	Reminders – To Do

Daily Reflection

Mood:

What emotion(s) did I feel?

What caused the emotion(s)?

What were my accomplishments?

Who am I? Really?

What did I learn today?

How can I improve tomorrow?

Daily Planner

M T W T F S S

Date:

Manifestation

Schedule

6:00	
7:00	
8:00	
9:00	
10:00	

Visualization

11:00	
12:00	
1:00	
2:00	
3:00	

Affirmation

4:00	
5:00	
6:00	
7:00	
8:00	
9:00	

Today, I am grateful for...	Inspired Actions & Priorities	Reminders - To Do

Daily Reflection

Mood:

What emotion(s) did I feel?

What caused the emotion(s)?

What were my accomplishments?

Who am I? Really?

What did I learn today?

How can I improve tomorrow?

Weekly Reflection

Date:

Where Am I Now?

Physical	Mental	Spiritual	Financial

Where Am I Going Next Week?

Physical	Mental	Spiritual	Financial

Weekly Reflection

Date: _____

What were my biggest accomplishments this week?

What lessons did I learn this week?

What have I been most grateful for this week?

What affirmations did I actualize this week?

How can I further realize my vision?

Weekly Planner

Date:

Manifestation

Schedule

Monday

Tuesday

Wednesday

Visualization

Thursday

Friday

Affirmation

Saturday

Sunday

Priorities	To Do

Weekly Mantra

555

I create Earth as it is in Heaven. I attract light and love into my life. People love being around me. I spread my love to others, and I watch as my love creates a ripple effect. Gradually, we raise the vibration of the world. We reach a frequency that is one with our Source and experience a reality that was first just a dream. In this present moment, I feel myself being one with the Universe. I feel my awareness bringing to me all that I desire to be. I create myself while at the same time creating others in my image of pure love and light.

Daily Planner

M T W T F S S

Date:

Manifestation

Visualization

Affirmation

Schedule

6:00	
7:00	
8:00	
9:00	
10:00	
11:00	
12:00	
1:00	
2:00	
3:00	
4:00	
5:00	
6:00	
7:00	
8:00	
9:00	

Today, I am grateful for...	Inspired Actions & Priorities	Reminders – To Do

Daily Reflection

Mood:

What emotion(s) did I feel?

What caused the emotion(s)?

What were my accomplishments?

Who am I? Really?

What did I learn today?

How can I improve tomorrow?

Daily Planner

M T W T F S S

Date:

Manifestation

Schedule

6:00	
7:00	
8:00	
9:00	
10:00	

Visualization

11:00	
12:00	
1:00	
2:00	
3:00	

Affirmation

4:00	
5:00	
6:00	
7:00	
8:00	
9:00	

Today, I am grateful for...	Inspired Actions & Priorities	Reminders – To Do

Daily Reflection

Mood:

What emotion(s) did I feel?

What caused the emotion(s)?

What were my accomplishments?

Who am I? Really?

What did I learn today?

How can I improve tomorrow?

Daily Planner

M T W T F S S

Date:

Manifestation

Schedule

6:00	
7:00	
8:00	
9:00	
10:00	
11:00	
12:00	
1:00	
2:00	
3:00	
4:00	
5:00	
6:00	
7:00	
8:00	
9:00	

Visualization

Affirmation

Today, I am grateful for...	Inspired Actions & Priorities	Reminders - To Do

Daily Reflection

Mood:

What emotion(s) did I feel?

What caused the emotion(s)?

What were my accomplishments?

Who am I? Really?

What did I learn today?

How can I improve tomorrow?

Daily Planner

M T W T F S S

Date:

Manifestation

Schedule

6:00	
7:00	
8:00	
9:00	
10:00	
11:00	
12:00	
1:00	
2:00	
3:00	
4:00	
5:00	
6:00	
7:00	
8:00	
9:00	

Visualization

Affirmation

Today, I am grateful for...	Inspired Actions & Priorities	Reminders – To Do

Daily Reflection

Mood:

What emotion(s) did I feel?

What caused the emotion(s)?

What were my accomplishments?

Who am I? Really?

What did I learn today?

How can I improve tomorrow?

Daily Planner

M T W T F S S

Date:

Manifestation

Schedule

6:00	
7:00	
8:00	
9:00	
10:00	
11:00	
12:00	
1:00	
2:00	
3:00	
4:00	
5:00	
6:00	
7:00	
8:00	
9:00	

Visualization

Affirmation

Today, I am grateful for...	Inspired Actions & Priorities	Reminders – To Do

Daily Reflection

Mood:

What emotion(s) did I feel?

What caused the emotion(s)?

What were my accomplishments?

Who am I? Really?

What did I learn today?

How can I improve tomorrow?

Daily Planner

M T W T F S S

Date:

Manifestation

Schedule

6:00	
7:00	
8:00	
9:00	
10:00	
11:00	
12:00	
1:00	
2:00	
3:00	
4:00	
5:00	
6:00	
7:00	
8:00	
9:00	

Visualization

Affirmation

Today, I am grateful for...	Inspired Actions & Priorities	Reminders - To Do

Daily Reflection

Mood:

What emotion(s) did I feel?

What caused the emotion(s)?

What were my accomplishments?

Who am I? Really?

What did I learn today?

How can I improve tomorrow?

Daily Planner

M T W T F S S

Date:

Manifestation

Visualization

Affirmation

Schedule

6:00	
7:00	
8:00	
9:00	
10:00	
11:00	
12:00	
1:00	
2:00	
3:00	
4:00	
5:00	
6:00	
7:00	
8:00	
9:00	

Today, I am grateful for...	Inspired Actions & Priorities	Reminders – To Do

Daily Reflection

Mood:

What emotion(s) did I feel?

What caused the emotion(s)?

What were my accomplishments?

Who am I? Really?

What did I learn today?

How can I improve tomorrow?

Weekly Reflection

Date:

Where Am I Now?

Physical	Mental	Spiritual	Financial

Where Am I Going Next Week?

Physical	Mental	Spiritual	Financial

Weekly Reflection

Date:

What were my biggest accomplishments this week?

What lessons did I learn this week?

What have I been most grateful for this week?

What affirmations did I actualize this week?

How can I further realize my vision?

Weekly Planner

Date:

Manifestation

Visualization

Affirmation

Schedule	
Monday	
Tuesday	
Wednesday	
Thursday	
Friday	
Saturday	
Sunday	

Priorities	To Do

Weekly Mantra

777

It's all happening for me. Every day, I wake up feeling lucky just for being who I am. I feel lucky for attracting all things good into my life. Feeling lucky is my natural state of being. I order something from the Universe and immediately get confirmation. I know who I am, and I know where I'm going. My destination is close, and I can feel it. I don't just think of my vision, I think from my vision. I live my life assuming my desire is already here, now. I act like my higher self, I walk like my higher self, and I talk like my higher self. I am my higher self.

Daily Planner

M T W T F S S

Date:

Manifestation

Schedule

6:00	
7:00	
8:00	
9:00	
10:00	
11:00	
12:00	
1:00	
2:00	
3:00	
4:00	
5:00	
6:00	
7:00	
8:00	
9:00	

Visualization

Affirmation

Today, I am grateful for...	Inspired Actions & Priorities	Reminders – To Do

Daily Reflection

Mood:

What emotion(s) did I feel?

What caused the emotion(s)?

What were my accomplishments?

Who am I? Really?

What did I learn today?

How can I improve tomorrow?

Daily Planner

M T W T F S S

Date:

Manifestation

Schedule

6:00	
7:00	
8:00	
9:00	
10:00	

Visualization

11:00	
12:00	
1:00	
2:00	
3:00	
4:00	

Affirmation

5:00	
6:00	
7:00	
8:00	
9:00	

Today, I am grateful for...	Inspired Actions & Priorities	Reminders – To Do

Daily Reflection

Mood:

What emotion(s) did I feel?

What caused the emotion(s)?

What were my accomplishments?

Who am I? Really?

What did I learn today?

How can I improve tomorrow?

Daily Planner

M T W T F S S

Date:

Manifestation

Schedule

6:00	
7:00	
8:00	
9:00	
10:00	

Visualization

11:00	
12:00	
1:00	
2:00	
3:00	

Affirmation

4:00	
5:00	
6:00	
7:00	
8:00	
9:00	

Today, I am grateful for...	Inspired Actions & Priorities	Reminders - To Do

Daily Reflection

Mood:

What emotion(s) did I feel?

What caused the emotion(s)?

What were my accomplishments?

Who am I? Really?

What did I learn today?

How can I improve tomorrow?

Daily Planner

M T W T F S S

Date:

Manifestation

Schedule

6:00	
7:00	
8:00	
9:00	
10:00	
11:00	
12:00	
1:00	
2:00	
3:00	
4:00	
5:00	
6:00	
7:00	
8:00	
9:00	

Visualization

Affirmation

Today, I am grateful for...	Inspired Actions & Priorities	Reminders – To Do

Daily Reflection

Mood:

What emotion(s) did I feel?

What caused the emotion(s)?

What were my accomplishments?

Who am I? Really?

What did I learn today?

How can I improve tomorrow?

Daily Planner

M T W T F S S

Date:

Manifestation

Schedule

6:00	
7:00	
8:00	
9:00	
10:00	
11:00	
12:00	
1:00	
2:00	
3:00	
4:00	
5:00	
6:00	
7:00	
8:00	
9:00	

Visualization

Affirmation

Today, I am grateful for...	Inspired Actions & Priorities	Reminders – To Do

Daily Reflection

Mood:

What emotion(s) did I feel?

What caused the emotion(s)?

What were my accomplishments?

Who am I? Really?

What did I learn today?

How can I improve tomorrow?

Daily Planner

M T W T F S S

Date:

Manifestation

Visualization

Affirmation

Schedule

6:00	
7:00	
8:00	
9:00	
10:00	
11:00	
12:00	
1:00	
2:00	
3:00	
4:00	
5:00	
6:00	
7:00	
8:00	
9:00	

Today, I am grateful for...	Inspired Actions & Priorities	Reminders - To Do

Daily Reflection

Mood:

What emotion(s) did I feel?

What caused the emotion(s)?

What were my accomplishments?

Who am I? Really?

What did I learn today?

How can I improve tomorrow?

Daily Planner

M T W T F S S

Date:

Manifestation

Schedule

6:00	
7:00	
8:00	
9:00	
10:00	

Visualization

11:00	
12:00	
1:00	
2:00	
3:00	

Affirmation

4:00	
5:00	
6:00	
7:00	
8:00	
9:00	

Today, I am grateful for...	Inspired Actions & Priorities	Reminders – To Do

Daily Reflection

Mood:

What emotion(s) did I feel?

What caused the emotion(s)?

What were my accomplishments?

Who am I? Really?

What did I learn today?

How can I improve tomorrow?

Weekly Reflection

Date:

Where Am I Now?

Physical	Mental	Spiritual	Financial

Where Am I Going Next Week?

Physical	Mental	Spiritual	Financial

Weekly Reflection

Date:

What were my biggest accomplishments this week?

What lessons did I learn this week?

What have I been most grateful for this week?

What affirmations did I actualize this week?

How can I further realize my vision?

Weekly Planner

Date:

Manifestation

Visualization

Affirmation

Schedule

Monday

Tuesday

Wednesday

Thursday

Friday

Saturday

Sunday

Priorities	To Do

Weekly Mantra

444

I learn to love two things very deeply. Myself and my creation. What I create for myself is what I create for others. I imagine this life as nothing more than a beautiful dance of creation. I learn to love the dance of creation. I am excited to see where it is taking me. I express myself freely and fully. I don't care what people think about me. What they think about me is nothing more than a perception of themselves, and how I react is my awareness of myself. I love my life and all aspects of my life.

Daily Planner

M T W T F S S

Date:

Manifestation

Schedule

6:00	
7:00	
8:00	
9:00	
10:00	

Visualization

11:00	
12:00	
1:00	
2:00	
3:00	
4:00	

Affirmation

5:00	
6:00	
7:00	
8:00	
9:00	

Today, I am grateful for...	Inspired Actions & Priorities	Reminders – To Do

Daily Reflection

Mood:

What emotion(s) did I feel?

What caused the emotion(s)?

What were my accomplishments?

Who am I? Really?

What did I learn today?

How can I improve tomorrow?

Daily Planner

M T W T F S S

Date:

Manifestation

Schedule

6:00	
7:00	
8:00	
9:00	
10:00	
11:00	
12:00	
1:00	
2:00	
3:00	
4:00	
5:00	
6:00	
7:00	
8:00	
9:00	

Visualization

Affirmation

Today, I am grateful for...	Inspired Actions & Priorities	Reminders - To Do

Daily Reflection

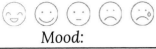

Mood:

What emotion(s) did I feel?

What caused the emotion(s)?

What were my accomplishments?

Who am I? Really?

What did I learn today?

How can I improve tomorrow?

Daily Planner

M T W T F S S

Date:

Manifestation

Schedule

6:00	
7:00	
8:00	
9:00	
10:00	
11:00	
12:00	
1:00	
2:00	
3:00	
4:00	
5:00	
6:00	
7:00	
8:00	
9:00	

Visualization

Affirmation

Today, I am grateful for...	Inspired Actions & Priorities	Reminders – To Do

Daily Reflection

Mood:

What emotion(s) did I feel?

What caused the emotion(s)?

What were my accomplishments?

Who am I? Really?

What did I learn today?

How can I improve tomorrow?

Daily Planner

M T W T F S S

Date:

Manifestation

Visualization

Affirmation

Schedule
6:00
7:00
8:00
9:00
10:00
11:00
12:00
1:00
2:00
3:00
4:00
5:00
6:00
7:00
8:00
9:00

Today, I am grateful for...	Inspired Actions & Priorities	Reminders - To Do

Daily Reflection

Mood:

What emotion(s) did I feel?

What caused the emotion(s)?

What were my accomplishments?

Who am I? Really?

What did I learn today?

How can I improve tomorrow?

Daily Planner

M T W T F S S

Date:

Manifestation

Visualization

Affirmation

Schedule

6:00	
7:00	
8:00	
9:00	
10:00	
11:00	
12:00	
1:00	
2:00	
3:00	
4:00	
5:00	
6:00	
7:00	
8:00	
9:00	

Today, I am grateful for...	Inspired Actions & Priorities	Reminders – To Do

Daily Reflection

Mood:

What emotion(s) did I feel?

What caused the emotion(s)?

What were my accomplishments?

Who am I? Really?

What did I learn today?

How can I improve tomorrow?

Daily Planner

M T W T F S S

Date:

Manifestation

Schedule

6:00	
7:00	
8:00	
9:00	
10:00	

Visualization

11:00	
12:00	
1:00	
2:00	
3:00	

Affirmation

4:00	
5:00	
6:00	
7:00	
8:00	
9:00	

Today, I am grateful for...	Inspired Actions & Priorities	Reminders - To Do

Daily Reflection

Mood:

What emotion(s) did I feel?

What caused the emotion(s)?

What were my accomplishments?

Who am I? Really?

What did I learn today?

How can I improve tomorrow?

Daily Planner

M T W T F S S

Date:

Manifestation

Schedule

6:00	
7:00	
8:00	
9:00	
10:00	
11:00	
12:00	
1:00	
2:00	
3:00	
4:00	
5:00	
6:00	
7:00	
8:00	
9:00	

Visualization

Affirmation

Today, I am grateful for...	Inspired Actions & Priorities	Reminders - To Do

Daily Reflection

Mood:

What emotion(s) did I feel?

What caused the emotion(s)?

What were my accomplishments?

Who am I? Really?

What did I learn today?

How can I improve tomorrow?

Weekly Reflection

Date:

Where Am I Now?

Physical	Mental	Spiritual	Financial

Where Am I Going Next Week?

Physical	Mental	Spiritual	Financial

Weekly Reflection

Date:

What were my biggest accomplishments this week?

What lessons did I learn this week?

What have I been most grateful for this week?

What affirmations did I actualize this week?

How can I further realize my vision?

Monthly Reflection

Month:

Top 10 Achievements

1. _____
2. _____
3. _____
4. _____
5. _____

6. _____
7. _____
8. _____
9. _____
10. _____

What have I been most grateful for this month?

What did I learn this month?

What obstacles did I face/overcome this month?

Monthly Reflection

Month:

Can I revise a specific scenario?

Where has my energy mostly been this month?

How can I improve for next month?

My Notes

My Notes

My Notes

My Notes

My Notes

My Notes

My Notes

My Notes

My Notes

My Notes

My Notes

My Notes

My Notes

My Notes

My Notes

My Notes

Self-Concept / Higher-Self

Date:

What are the habits associated with your higher self?

My higher self embodies waking up and going to sleep at the same time every day. My higher self eats healthy and exercises regularly. My higher self meditates for at least 30 minutes every day. My higher self works for at least 6 hours a day.

What are the activities associated with your higher self?

My higher self reads and writes for at least an hour a day. My higher self goes to the gym 5-6 times a week. My higher self loves to jog, go on long walks, Sun-gaze, and ground on Earth. My higher self loves networking while maintaining a state of balance.

What are the qualities associated with your higher self?

My higher self is kind and filled with love. My higher self is funny and makes everyone laugh. My higher self has an amazing work ethic. My higher self is confident in all that he does. My higher self is generous and humble. My higher self is filled with gratitude.

How would you visualize yourself embodying that new you?

I visualize my higher self by seeing him communicating with such immense vocabulary. I see my higher self closing a $50 Million Dollar Deal. I see my higher self giving back to his community and loved ones. I see my higher self celebrating all of his successes.

I embrace and obtain the same activities, habits, and qualities associated with my higher self. I no longer associate my future with my past. I declare at this present moment, I am one with my higher self, and my higher self is in harmony with my vision.

Evolving Into Your Higher Self

	WHERE ARE YOU NOW?	WHERE ARE YOU GOING?
HEALTH & WELLNESS	I am currently 230 lbs with 16% bodyfat. I sometimes catch myself eating foods I shouldn't be eating. I go out drinking 3-4 times a week and also party on the weekends. I currently smoke a pack a day.	I am 200 lbs with 13% bodyfat. I am eating healthy and cooking my own meals. I exercise 5-6 times a week and only go out on special occasions. I only drink responsibly and only when I am out. I live a healthy smoke-free life.
SPIRITUAL & MENTAL	I currently meditate or pray once or twice a week. I practice sungazing and grounding on the weekends but I sometimes forget. I let the judgement of others effect me and sometimes I get sad at situations.	I meditate and pray every single day. I sun gaze and practice grounding 4-5 times a week. I practice gratitude for having everything I need in my life every day. I stay positive. I see hardships as opportunity and I don't let others effect me in any way.
BUSINESS & OCCUPATION	I am currently working as a director for a marketing agency. I do side jobs every now and then and try to learn new ways to make passive income.	I own my own marketing agency. I have 3-5 employees that help me prospect and gather new clients. We are in the growing stage and this is just the beginning.
WEALTH & PROSPERITY	I am making $4,000 a month. When I work really hard with side jobs I can make a little over $5,000 a month. My company provides me with people who need help with their ads.	I am making $10,000 a month. $1,500 of that is passive income. I opened my first company and we have already gotten over 100 new clients!

Self-Realization

Who are you? Where are you going?
I am a hard worker, capable of anything. I am one with the highest and I treat others how I treat myself. I am successful, loving, caring, honest, and prosperous. I am becoming the best version of myself. I am going to open a new company and it is going to help thousands of people.

What is your purpose? What is your passion?
My purpose is to help people scale their businesses. My purpose is forever evolving into something more significant, and further realizing new visions. My passion is creating ads that convert well. My passion is seeing people happy with the value I have to offer.

What are you the most grateful for in your life?
I am most grateful for my family, my loved ones, my capability to create, my food, my home, my bed, the ground I walk upon, the bridge of incidents, my creation, my being, my presence, my oneness with God, my healthy lifestyle, my income, my heart, my love, and my opportunity to provide service to others.

What does your dream life look like?
My dream life is full of love, prosperity, and abundance. I am traveling the world, giving and receiving money on autopilot every single day. I live in a beautiful home with my loving family. I am further opening new businesses and seeing how else I can further help others.

I AM grateful for receiving all that I desire. I live my dream life regardless of what my senses tell me. It's already done; I rise in consciousness to the state in which my desire has been met. I claim, Creation is complete. I am that I am.

Opposites Attract

RESISTANCE	WHAT'S THE CAUSE?	OPPOSITE
Making YouTube videos	I need to know all of the answers	I don't need to know all of the answers.
Opening a new business.	It won't succeed	It will succeed
Entering a new relationship.	My partner won't appreciate what I have to offer.	My partner knows my worth. My partner knows I am valuable and therefore is grateful for what I have to offer.
Networking with new people.	They will say no to my service.	They will say yes to my service because I know that my service is valuable and can help them 10x their company!

I polarize in consciousness to the desired state. My natural state of consciousness is one with confidence, faith, conviction, love, and presence of mind. I am that I am.

Monthly Planner

Month:

	Monday	Tuesday	Wednesday
Priorities			
Drop off check to my boss's office.	Meeting at 1PM	Marina's birthday	
Pay rent			
Make new content			
Follow up with Andi			
Habits			
Reading	Meeting at 1PM	Date Night	John's birthday
Writing			
meditating			
exercising			
waking up early		Go to post office	Meeting at 3PM
Intentions			
Helping others			
Giving			
Being kind	Meeting at 1PM	Date Night	
Spreading awareness.			

Monthly Manifestation	Visualization	Affirmation
I am opening my second business.	I see myself filled with excitement and joy. I see the website already made and clients already signing up.	I am opening a 7 figure business that will help people and their companies grow to their max potential.

Monthly Planner

Month:

Thursday	Friday	Saturday	Sunday
	Family time 2-10 Study and learn		Open House
Date Night			Open House
	Family time 2-10		Jessica's birthday Open House
Meet up with Chris			Open House
	Family time 2-10		Open House

Notes

Alignment Tracker

Month:

Monday	Tuesday	Wednesday	Thursday	Friday	Saturday	Sunday

Morning Routine:
Wake up at 6, Stretch, Jog, Clean up / Organize, Exercise /
Gym, 30 minutes of reading, 15 minutes of writing, Meditate,
Cold Shower, Work and Emails

Visualization:
I see myself waking up every morning full of energy and
excited to get started with my day. I feel great cleaning the
environment around me. I see myself losing weight and being
more productive. I see myself taking a cold shower and feeling
the water run through me.

Affirmation:
I am creative, I am persistent, I have ultimate willpower. I am
committed, I am passionate, and I am loved. I have an
abundance of energy, my thoughts are positive, and I am
extremely focused. I am healthy, I am wealthy, I am wise. I am
smart, I am successful, I am that I am!

Alignment Tracker

Month: _____

How do you feel going into next month?
I am incredibly excited going into next month. I have
opportunities lined up for me. My income is increasing, and I am
persistent towards my goals. Next month is going to be a
breakthrough. I feel and claim next month is the month!

What are the habits, activities, and behaviors to unlearn?
Quit smoking. Quit going on my phone first thing in the morning.
Quit leaving stuff around and not cleaning up after myself.

_____

_____

What are the habits, activities, and behaviors to improve on?
Staying consistent with stretching. Implement yoga to help me
improve.

_____

_____

What are the new habits, activities, and behaviors to master?
Drink a gallon of water a day. Be conscious of everything I put in
my body.

_____

_____

I am rising in consciousness to the naturalness of the thing desired.
I am whatever I say I am. Therefore I declare, My journey is just
as rewarding as the destination. I am becoming the best version of
myself. I am certain creation is finished. It is done. It's already
mine.

Weekly Planner

Date:

Manifestation

I am getting $10,000

in total sales this

Week.

Visualization

I can see the sales.

I see and feel myself

myself excited and

celebrating my wins.

Affirmation

I am grateful for

$10,000 in sales this

week. I am abundant,

smart, and prosperous.

Schedule

Monday

Tuesday

Wednesday

Thursday

Friday

Saturday

Sunday

Priorities	To Do
Create new content Follow up with my marketing team.	Go to home depot. Drop off check to my boss.

Daily Planner

M T W T F S S

Date:

Manifestation

I am creating a viral

post today.

_____

_____

Visualization

The views and likes are

rolling in. Everyone is

loving my content!

_____

Affirmation

I am grateful for all

the views and likes. I

have valuable content

that everyone enjoys.

Schedule

Time	
6:00	
7:00	
8:00	
9:00	
10:00	
11:00	
12:00	
1:00	
2:00	
3:00	
4:00	
5:00	
6:00	
7:00	
8:00	
9:00	

Today, I am grateful for...	Inspired Actions & Priorities	Reminders - To Do
Waking up in the morning My loved ones My ability to create	Creating content. Researching tips and tricks on content creation.	Follow up with clients Call attorney Dani's Birthday

Daily Reflection

Mood:

What emotion(s) did I feel?
Happy in the morning.
A little bit frustrated
Towards the end of
my content creation.

What caused the emotion(s)?
I completed my morning
routine, it made me feel
great. Towards the end
I got frustrated and
redid all of my content.

What were my accomplishments?
I completed my morning
ritual. I made my bed,
cleaned, got organized,
and made three videos.

Who am I? Really?
I AM divine perfection.
I AM one with the highest.
I am loving listening.
I am a successful business
owner. I AM in-spirit.

What did I learn today?
I learned new tips for
marketing and creating
new content.

How can I improve tomorrow?
Breathwork in the morning.
Read after working out.
Be patient and relaxed.
Ask someone for help if I
need it. It's okay.

Weekly Reflection

Date:

Where Am I Now?

Physical	Mental	Spiritual	Financial
220 lbs 15% Bodyfat. I exercised 4 times this past week.	I am feeling great. I am more focused, aligned, and inspired in all areas of my life.	I meditated and prayed everyday the past week. I am sungazing everyday. I go out in nature for grounding, and earthing once a week.	I hit my $10,000 week in sales! Savings are at $205,000

Where Am I Going Next Week?

Physical	Mental	Spiritual	Financial
215 lbs 14.5% Bodyfat. Exercise 5 times a week. Jog and stretch everyday.	I am inspired and inspiring the people around me. Negative thoughts don't effect me.	I meditate and pray every day. My awareness is strong, and I am always mindful.	I am hitting $15,000 in weekly sales. Savings will be at $210,000

Weekly Reflection

Date:

What were my biggest accomplishments this week?
I hit $15,000 for the week.

I have been staying true to my morning routine.

I have been clean and organized.

I got a new business deal.

What lessons did I learn this week?
I learned new breathwork techniques.

I learned more tips on content creation.

I figured out a new marketing strategy.

What have I been most grateful for this week?
My family and my loved ones. My dog, my bed, my food.

The support I get from everyone watching my content.

My capacity to manifest anything I desire.

My loyalty to the unseen reality.

What affirmations did I actualize this week?
I AM forgiving. I forgave myself for a mistake that I made.

I AM inspired (in-spirit). I am constantly enthusiastic and happy while I continue this beautiful journey. I AM prosperous.

My value got me $15,000 in sales this week.

How can I further realize my vision?
Create at least five pieces of content per week.

Continue watching tutorials and videos for marketing and content.

Focus on the value of the content. Don't overthink it.

Listen to the hunches of my inner voice. My intuition guides me.

Monthly Reflection

Month: _____

Top 10 Achievements

1. Launched a new product
2. Connected with new people
3. Consistent morning routine
4. Lost 10lbs
5. 8 minute mile

6. Passed my exam
7. Drank a gallon of water a day
8. Made my bed every morning
9. Meditated every day
10. New opportunities

What have I been most grateful for this month?

I am grateful for hitting 100K last month. I am grateful for my mentor.

I am grateful for my family and loved ones. I am grateful for having the

opportunity to create. I am grateful for my divine awareness.

I am grateful for waking up. I am grateful for love.

What did I learn this month?

I learned that I love who I am. I learned that everything happens

for a reason. I learned to accept and let go of things that no longer

serve me. I learned to love being alone; just me and my creation.

What obstacles did I face/overcome this month?

I faced the hardship of smoking. I overcame it with the love of my being.

The love of who I AM and who I will always return to.

I take my attention away from instant gratification. Instead,

I realize because gratification is my natural state of being.

Monthly Reflection

Month:

Can I revise a specific scenario?

Here, you write your revised story. Write it as if it happened the way you would have desired it to go.

Where has my energy mostly been this month?

I have been channeling my energy into my work, my success, my health, and my learning. I only channel my energy into things that benefit me and my being. I am aware of where my energy goes.

How can I improve for next month?

Stay consistent, persist in the feeling of the wish fulfilled.

Stay on track with my morning routine, stay organized and clean.

Enjoy the journey in flow, where doubt and fear do not exist.

Detach myself from any outcome, enjoy being in the present moment.